Cell Phones
Don't Work
in Heaven

Cell Phones Don't Work in Heaven

So Let's Talk Now:
Documenting and
Preserving Your
Family's Asset$

By Mark C. Pope IV
with Barbara R. Thompson

Published and distributed by Pope Publishing, LLC
8575 Cobb International Blvd.
Kennesaw, GA 30152

Co-author and editor: Barbara R. Thompson
barbrthompson@gmail.com

Illustrations © 2012 Roger Fleming
Book Designer: Roger Fleming
www.HeyRoger.com

Cover Designer: Laurie Shock
www.ShockDesignBooks.com

Printed by Graphic Solutions Group, Kennesaw, GA, USA
www.gsghome.com/

First Edition

ISBN13 978-0-615-51513-7
Library of Congress Catalog Number 2012901392

A portion of the proceeds from *Cell Phones Don't Work in Heaven* goes to support our favorite nonprofits. For more information and links to these worthy organizations, see our website: www.cellphonesdontworkinheaven.com.

Special Sales/Bulk Sales/Premiums
For information about bulk sales for nonprofits, civic groups, book clubs, faith communities, extended families, and other organizations, please contact Mark Pope at popepub@gsghome.com.

www.cellphonesdontworkinheaven.com

DEDICATION

To all the men and women who, regardless of what life throws at them, want to give financial protection to their families. Ralph, a good friend of mine, contends life has the best curveball he has ever seen.

And closer to home and heart, I dedicate this book to the love of my life, my wife, Chilton, and our children. All of them have been my inspiration, and all of them have always made me proud.

TABLE OF CONTENTS

Quick Reference

Alphabetical List of Forms and Worksheets

Acknowledgments

I would like to thank Barbara Thompson for her "heavy editing," for her belief in the project, and most importantly for occasionally reining in the sometimes irreverent observations produced by my friend Ralph and me about life's most difficult subjects. Without her help, moral support, and subtle and not-so-subtle guidance, this book never would have been completed.

I'd like to thank book designer and cartoonist Roger Fleming for his unusual ability to illustrate a rather somber subject with just the right amount of irreverent humor. Over many lunches with Barbara and me, he never lost his patience or his creativity.

We are all indebted to Laurie Shock, whose skill and talent for book design is without peer and whose contributions to content and style were invaluable. We also want to thank Bob Land for his careful proofreading, a skill he has raised to an art form.

PART ONE
INTRODUCTION

"I told you cell phones don't work in heaven."

ONE

WAKE-UP CALL

Cell Phones Don't Work in Heaven BEGAN WITH A WAKE-UP CALL, the kind that arrives without warning and rearranges the pieces of your life.

It was a perfect fall day in South Georgia, and I was at a hunting club shooting wild quail with friends. I had it all planned out: a pleasant afternoon in the field, dinner and drinks, a night at the lodge, and an early return to work in Atlanta.

I was with a guide and some customers, all of whom had hunted their entire lives. Although I enjoy watching bird dogs work the field, I am not the best shot and was completely surprised when, in the first group we flushed, I hit a bird. I went over to pick it up, and as I walked back to the group, I remember thinking, "This is not a good idea." I was breaking one of the cardinal rules of hunting. I could not see every hunter in our group, and they could not see me.

I heard the frantic flutter of wild quail taking flight, and the next thing I knew, I was on my knees, with my gun in the mud. Blood was pouring from my face, and I felt like I had been punched by a nail gun. There was a tremendous pressure in my chest.

"I've been hit!"

At the same moment, one of my best customers shouted, "I got one!"

> This was one of the first times in my life that I heard the voice of my wise and insightful alter ego, Ralph, who you will meet many times in the pages of this book. "Thank the Lord you said *I've been hit*," he observed approvingly. "That's what John Wayne would have yelled. He would never say *I've been shot*."

"Yeah!" the guide yelled. "And you got Pope, too."

As if in slow motion, I pulled my gun out of the mud and sat down. I felt as if there was a hurricane whirling in my head. I knew that I had to hold the storm right where it was so that it wouldn't take over, and that's just what I did. In that split second, when I did not know if I was dead or alive, an enormous sense of peace and well-being washed over me. I did not think about the past or the future, and I felt that if I died right then, it would be okay. There was nothing to be afraid of.

This awareness, with its absolute certainty, stayed with me through some delicate moments in the hospital—a bullet had lodged in my heart—and it remains with me to this day. Everything is going to be okay.

Over the years, my hunting accident has morphed into one of the funniest stories I tell. Why, for example, was everyone so shaken that they allowed me to drive back to the car and then drive the car to the hospital? And what about the puzzled and alarmed technician who was not told why I needed X-rays of my chest? He asked me if I ever had been shot before. I said no, thinking he meant prior to my accident, and he gave me an odd look. Later when I told him that I had been in a hunting accident that very day, he said, "Thank the Lord, Mr. Pope, because you have buckshot in you, and I didn't think you knew how it got there!"

But there was a serious side as well. It was a reminder that "It can't happen to me" was just a myth I told myself. It was a timing issue only. Sooner or later, something was going to happen to me, to all of us. It was a question of what and when, not if.

One Monday night after the accident, I was sitting at my desk in a reflective mood, thinking about my wife—the love of my life—and my children. What would our future be, I wondered, both as individuals and as a family? Yes, if something happened to me, they would all be okay in the long term. But what about

Who Is Ralph?

Ralph is a good if irreverent friend of the author who has resided in the bottom left-hand corner of his brain and the right, top part of his heart since 1968. Ralph hangs onto reality only by a small thread of conservative upbringing.

Unlike me, Ralph never has to deal with the outside world, so he can speak his mind with no downside. He is the devil's advocate, sarcastic wit, doubting Thomas, and mischievous man-child in me that yearns to be heard. He brings a smile to my inner self almost every day when he fires off a brutally honest assessment of what someone has said or done. He's usually dead-on.

He also needs to be filtered. Unlike Ralph, I do have to deal with the outside world, and I cannot always afford to share Ralph's lightning-fast opinions. Good manners and hard-earned judgment don't usually allow his thoughts to get past my vocal cords. My wonderful wife of thirty-eight years taught me this lesson almost forty years ago.

Everybody has a Ralph living inside. It just depends on whether you let him out now and again for a stroll.

the chaos that would surely follow the first days and weeks of my absence? How would they find the critical information and financial resources they needed? Who would they turn to for advice?

And then there was the question of my hard-earned assets. Was there any way to make sure that they would be distributed, protected, and preserved according to my wishes? Would the people who were advising my family have the professional and moral qualifications to help them through a difficult transition? One thing was certain: Unless I made a written plan—and who better to make this plan than me?—there were no guarantees.

I grabbed a pencil and that yellow pad and began writing. The more I wrote, the more information I realized I needed to provide. Bank account numbers, the location of my will, the names and contact information for lawyers and accountants. Did I want my family to sell or hold our business? What about the valuable print hanging in my office? And who would be my family's advisors *when*, not *if*—that sobering, cold-shower thought again— I was gone?

They were largely questions that only I could answer, and in a very short time I was able to organize all the information that I felt my family needed. The result: an absolutely essential document for my wife and children and a deep sense of peace and satisfaction for me.

This book has been written for you and your loved ones, to help you move toward that sense of relief and confidence that comes from taking charge of your personal affairs. The reflections and worksheets that follow will enable you to quickly and efficiently organize your family's "essential book of information." You can do it alone or with a family member. If you are buying this book for a spouse or partner, why not sit down one Sunday afternoon, with a cup of coffee in hand, and fill it out together? The reward will be not only your own peace of mind but the knowledge that you will have helped guide your loved ones through one of the most difficult and perilous transitions of their lives.

By the way, all the stories I tell about myself in this guide are true. I've modified a few details to protect the innocent and not-so-innocent—including myself.

TWO

How to Use This Book

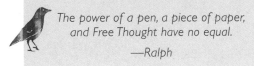

The power of a pen, a piece of paper, and Free Thought have no equal.

—Ralph

THIS BOOK IS COMPOSED OF TWO PARTS: (1) guidelines and reflections with some important tools for calculating your family's Green $tream, and (2) worksheets that make it easy to give your loved ones the vital information they need. These forms can be filled out with the most critical information in a single afternoon. Just pull up a chair with your spouse, get a cup of coffee or glass of wine, and begin in any order that helps you get going.

Perhaps you want to start with the view from 30,000 feet, giving sage advice as directed on page 68. Perhaps you feel most comfortable simply writing down where your will can be found or listing your credit cards. In that case, turn to pages 14–15 and 85. The most important thing is to get started. Just remember to be as specific as possible and give explanatory details where necessary.

There are some special subjects covered by the guidelines and accompanying worksheets that will be more important to you than others. Take a minute to look over the table of contents in the front of the book and the alphabetical list of forms found on page viii. If you are a pet owner, you will want to read chapter 27 and fill out the forms on pages 131–132. If you own a business, be sure to read chapter 29 and look at the forms beginning on page 138.

The most important information you can leave your family is the answer to the question: WHERE are your vital documents located? Space is provided for additional information where helpful, but don't delay recording the location of your documents by getting bogged down in providing too much information. If you make this project too big and time consuming, you might not get it done at all.

Here's to a smooth journey and a significant reward at the finish line: a sense of accomplishment and the peace of mind that results from taking care of your own affairs and the affairs of those you love.

THREE

SECURITY CHECK

NOW'S THE TIME TO MAKE A SIMPLE PLAN to keep this book secure from theft and out of the hands of relatives with NBS—Nosy Beneficiary Syndrome. And by the way, it IS contagious. I know. I've seen it, and I've had it. Haven't you? Be honest, now.

On one big-hearted hand, you are filling out this book because you want your family to have quick access to the confidential information inside. On the other, more street-smart hand, you want it to be on your time schedule, not theirs.

So come up with a simple plan to secure the completed book and to let a trusted individual or individuals know where it is. If you're like me, simple plans are the only ones you can come up with anyway.

If just you and your spouse know the whereabouts of *Cell Phones Don't Work in Heaven*, remember to have a backup plan in case something happens to both of you. One option is to give your lawyer or a bank trust department a key to a lockbox that contains the book. Be sure to tell a trusted individual what you've done. The bottom line: make sure *Cell Phones Don't Work in Heaven* is secure but accessible when needed.

What's with the Raven?

The raven is a mystical symbol of the afterlife, a messenger between the next world and the one we like to perceive as terra firma. Although as I think about it, the raven could also be the connection between you and your midlife crisis, or between your "full throttle, baby" and "whoa, baby" selves or whatever other selves you know are there but resist direct contact.

I like what I've written here; I just don't understand it. Maybe that's the point. . . .

Now, turn the doggone page and fill out the most important form for the day after your last day.

Just do it!
—Ralph

Part Two
First Steps

"Can you ask him where he wants to be buried?"

FOUR

THE DAY AFTER YOUR LAST DAY

In the hours and days immediately following your departure from Mother Earth, your family is going to need quick access to the names and numbers of some of the important professional players in your life.

Clergy

Name

Email   Phone Number

Address

Funeral Directives

Location of documents

Funeral Home

Name

Email   Phone Number

Address

Financial Advisor

Name

Email   Phone Number

Address

THE DAY AFTER YOUR LAST DAY

Life Insurance Agent

Name

Email   Phone Number

Address

Accountant/Tax Preparer

Name

Email   Phone Number

Address

Attorney

Name

Email   Phone Number

Address

Tax Returns/Documents

Location of documents

Social Security Card and Statement

Location of documents

FIVE

WHY A WILL ISN'T ENOUGH

You can't put everything in your will that your family needs to know when you're history.

—Ralph

HAROLD WAS A SUCCESSFUL FINANCIAL ADVISOR and a whiz at estate planning. When it came to his own wife, children, and grandchildren, he made sure he had covered all the bases: a will, trusts for the grandchildren, plenty of life insurance, and a funeral that was already paid for. The day after he died, however, his wife was in a panic. She had only half listened when he had talked about financial matters. Now, in her grief, she could not remember where to find the will and which items among his personal possessions he wanted to give to his children and grandchildren. Worse, she didn't know how to access a critical bank account, and she wasn't even sure if she could cover her current monthly expenses. Under pressure from a well-meaning but ill-advised friend, she withdrew money early from a retirement account and paid a stiff penalty.

It is an all-too-familiar story. Even with what seems to be adequate advance planning, a husband or wife, adult child or sibling, is left behind to address serious financial and family issues in an emotionally charged state—and without adequate information. In the midst of pain and confusion, otherwise sensible people (and some not so sensible) too often make serious mistakes, including listening to poor advice.

Sooner or later, and ready or not, you, too, are going to leave behind loved ones to take care of your—now their—affairs. You can choose to let them fend for themselves and struggle on their own through the massive reorganization of their lives. Or, by simply taking a few hours, you can help them successfully navigate a complicated and trying emotional situation.

This book has been designed to make it easy for you to talk with your family about genuinely difficult things. No matter what your age, whether you are single or married, with children or without, the pages that follow will help you provide your loved ones with the essential information they will need for safe passage to the next stage of their lives.

This is not a book about financial strategy, estate planning, writing a will, or creating a trust. Everyone, whatever their financial status, needs these tools—but not from me. I don't give stock tips or advice on golf swings either. As a 17 handicap, I'm the recipient of pointers from well-intentioned golfers who keep losing money with me as their partner. But here is an important fact that you need to know about a will or trust. It is the underlying reason why I am writing this book, and I hope it will be a driving force for you to fill it out for your loved ones. **You can't put everything in your will or trust that your family needs to know when you're gone.** Single, married, or divorced, it doesn't matter. **Wills, trusts, and other legal documents are simply not designed to communicate some of the most important information your family needs.** For instance:

- Where IS the original of your will, and what is the name of the lawyer who drew it up?
- Are there life insurance policies? If so, where are they located and who are the insurance agents?
- What are your assets and income streams? Debts and liabilities?
- How much money will your partner or spouse have to live on after you are gone?
- Who really gets the portrait of Great-grandpa—and why?

Do these sound like simple questions with straightforward answers? To confirm that they are not, talk to some friends about how it feels to search high and low through their parents' home looking for a will that is nowhere to be found. Listen to spouses who, in the middle of paralyzing grief, realize that they do not know if they have enough money to cover their monthly expenses. Try settling an escalating argument between two otherwise civilized family members, both of whom believe that they were promised their grandmother's antique mirror.

All these matters are legitimate concerns that deserve well-planned answers, and who better qualified to give them than you?

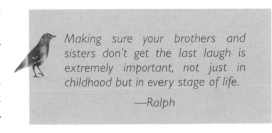

Making sure your brothers and sisters don't get the last laugh is extremely important, not just in childhood but in every stage of life.

—Ralph

Remember, if you don't do it, others who are less informed and who may even have agendas of their own will do it for you. Life will be moving on, your family will still need important information from you, and you will not be there. If you're counting on communicating with your family through a séance or mystical medium, then put this book down and get a refund; I've lost you.

Okay, you're still reading. It's a good sign that you're buying into the program. Because that's what it is—a living, breathing, evolving document that requires updating for the rest of what hopefully will be a long, illustrious, and love-filled life. While the subject matter can be initially unsettling, the reward is enormous. As part of your legacy, you will be supporting your family members and influencing their affairs at one of the most critical and difficult stages of their lives.

While you are at it, why not give a copy of **Cell Phones Don't Work in Heaven** to the other significant people in your life? Parents, spouse or partner, adult children, siblings—they all can be encouraged to record their vital information. And why let any more time elapse before you ask your loved ones to record the information that only they possess, but that you will someday need?

Think about that brother or sister, younger or older, whose messes you have cleaned up for years, whose lack of organization has caused you one headache after

> The words *spouse, family member,* and *partner* are used interchangeably, but it is also possible that someone else not related to the deceased, such as a family friend or lawyer, could be settling the estate.

another. Do you really want that person to get the last laugh by forcing you once again to unravel and interpret their mosaic lifestyle so you can settle their affairs? Providing your siblings with their own workbooks will not only save you time and effort down the road, but you will also have the contentment of knowing that your slack brother or sister has had to put some effort into organizing his or her own life.

SIX

Your Wills and Trusts: Where Are They?

If you can't justify a bequest to yourself, maybe it's not such a brilliant idea after all.

—Ralph

A WILL ISN'T ENOUGH, BUT IT IS ABSOLUTELY essential. This is one document that you can't live without, and it's important to update it periodically throughout your life. If you don't have a will because you're waiting to write it another day, remember: Your assets ARE going to be redistributed, one way or another. Either the court will follow the guidelines in your will or the court will make decisions for you. Your way or their way. I rest my case.

Take a moment to reflect on potential areas of confusion and conflict in your own family concerning your will. On the pages provided here, spell out your intentions explicitly. Explain how you want complicated matters handled. Clarify and give background information. Write down everything it takes to ensure that family members understand your feelings and intentions.

Now is the time to explain to your family members otherwise mysterious provisions in your will. Don't leave everyone wondering why you have bequeathed half of your assets to the Dalai Lama or the Whale Sharks Have Feelings Too foundation. Why not explain the thought process behind your decision?

My Will

Date _____

Original Will

Location _____

_____

_____

Copies of Will

Location _____

_____

_____

Explanations and additional information concerning my will

_____

_____

_____

_____

_____

_____

_____

_____

_____

_____

_____

_____

MY WILL

Explanations and additional information concerning my will

My Trusts

Date _____

Trust Number One

Title of Trust _____

Attorney's Law Firm _____

Email _____ Phone Number _____

Address _____

_____

Location of Copies of Trust _____

_____

Name _____ Phone Number _____

Address _____

_____

Additional Contact Information (if needed) _____

_____

Explanations and additional information concerning this trust

_____

_____

_____

_____

_____

_____

_____

_____

MY TRUSTS

Date _____

Trust Number Two

Title of Trust _____

Attorney's Law Firm _____

Email _____ Phone Number _____

Address _____

_____

Location of Copies of Trust _____

_____

Name _____ Phone Number _____

Address _____

_____

Additional Contact Information (if needed) _____

_____

Explanations and additional information concerning this trust

_____

_____

_____

_____

_____

_____

_____

_____

MY TRUSTS

Date

Trust Number Three

Title of Trust

Attorney's Law Firm

Email   Phone Number

Address

Location of Copies of Trust

Name   Phone Number

Address

Additional Contact Information (if needed)

Explanations and additional information concerning this trust

SEVEN

Advance Directives

It is never too early to make your end-of-life wishes known— but it can be too late.

—Ralph

ADVANCE HEALTH-CARE DIRECTIVES ARE ABSOLUTELY ESSENTIAL documents for all of us to put in place—and the sooner the better. They will speak for us when we can no longer speak for ourselves and save our family members from potentially heartwrenching decisions at a helpless and confusing time.

Each state has its own laws regarding advance directives, so a little research is in order. The Mayo Clinic provides an explanation of the documents you need at www.mayoclinic.com/health/living-wills/HA00014.

For a clear, comprehensive, and user-friendly approach to making a living will, it's hard to do better than the *Five Wishes* documents produced by Aging with Dignity. Visit their website: www.agingwithdignity.org/five-wishes.php, or call 1-888-5-WISHES (1-888-594-7437). The five wishes are:

- Who you want to make health-care decisions for you when you can't
- The kind of medical treatment you want or don't want
- How comfortable you want to be
- How you want people to treat you
- What you want your loved ones to know

Some friendly advice: Don't put off making your wishes known!

Five Wishes

Five Wishes can also help you choose your health-care agent—the person who will make the critical decisions regarding medical care and life support when you are in the end stages of your life. **Choose carefully**: the best person is definitely not a family member short of cash, nor is it necessarily any family member, including your spouse— although of course it might be.

As the authors of *Five Wishes* note, you alone know the right person to be in charge here. They recommend choosing someone who is nearby; can stand up for you so that your wishes are followed; is able to be both assertive and courteous; and will agree, in conversation with you, to follow your wishes.

ADVANCE DIRECTIVES

Note to Reader

Advance directives include a living will, a Do Not Resuscitate (DNR) order, and a medical or healthcare power of attorney designation.

Date _____

Location(s) of All Advance Directive Documents*

Name _____

Email _____ Phone Number _____

Address _____

Name _____

Email _____ Phone Number _____

Address _____

Medical or Health-Care Power of Attorney

Name _____

Email _____ Phone Number _____

Address _____

*You will want these documents in the hands of the person who has medical power of attorney, as well as filed with your physicians, and easily available to your family members.

EIGHT

Family Legal Papers

CONGRATULATIONS! YOU ARE WELL under way. Below and in the pages that follow, you will have the chance to quickly capture the basic information your family needs about legal papers, passwords, locks and lockboxes, mortgages, and insurance.

Date

Location of Documents

Adoption

Annulment

Automobiles

Birth Certificate

Boats

Divorce

Immigration and Naturalization

Marriage Certificate

Memberships and Season Tickets

Military Records

Passport and Travel Papers

Prenuptial Agreements

Property Deeds and Surveys

Social Security Cards / Statements

NINE

Home Mortgages

Date

Location of Documents

Primary Mortgage

Address

Original Loan Amount   Interest Rate

Monthly Payment Due Date

Terms

Other Information

Second Mortgage

Address

Original Loan Amount   Interest Rate

Monthly Payment Due Date

Terms

Other Information

HOME MORTGAGES

Date _____

Location of Documents _____

_____

First Mortgage on Home Number Two

Address _____

_____

Original Loan Amount _____ Interest Rate _____

Monthly Payment Due Date _____

Terms _____

_____

Other Information _____

_____

Second Mortgage on Home Number Two

Address _____

_____

Original Loan Amount _____ Interest Rate _____

Monthly Payment Due Date _____

Terms _____

_____

Other Information _____

_____

INSURANCE POLICIES

Date _____

Location of Documents _____

_____

Corporate Life Insurance / Disability

Name of Company / Agent _____

Policy Number / Amount _____

Policy Renewal Date _____

Disability Insurance

Name of Company / Agent _____

Policy Number / Amount _____

Policy Renewal Date _____

Earthquake Insurance

Name of Company / Agent _____

Policy Number / Amount _____

Policy Renewal Date _____

INSURANCE POLICIES

*You don't need them
Until you need them
But when you need them
You REALLY need them
So don't neglect them
Or forget them
I promise you
Your family members will thank you.*

—Ralph

Date

Location of Documents

Flood Insurance

Name of Company / Agent

Policy Number / Amount

Policy Renewal Date

Health Insurance Policy Number One

Name of Company / Agent

Policy Number / Amount

Policy Renewal Date

Health Insurance Policy Number Two

Name of Company / Agent

Policy Number / Amount

Policy Renewal Date

INSURANCE POLICIES

Date

Location of Documents

Health Insurance Supplemental Policy

Name of Company / Agent

Policy Number / Amount

Policy Renewal Date

Home and Land Insurance Policy Number One

Name of Company / Agent

Policy Number / Amount

Policy Renewal Date

Home and Land Insurance Policy Number Two

Name of Company / Agent

Policy Number / Amount

Policy Renewal Date

Life Insurance Policy Number One

Name of Company / Agent

Policy Number / Amount

Policy Renewal Date

INSURANCE POLICIES

Date

Location of Documents

Life Insurance Policy Number Two

Name of Company / Agent

Policy Number / Amount

Policy Renewal Date

Long-term Care

Name of Company / Agent

Policy Number / Amount

Policy Renewal Date

Travel Insurance

Name of Company / Agent

Policy Number / Amount

Policy Renewal Date

Umbrella Policy

Name of Company / Agent

Policy Number / Amount

Policy Renewal Date

INSURANCE POLICIES

Date

Location of Documents

Wind / Hurricane Insurance

Name of Company / Agent

Policy Number / Amount

Policy Renewal Date

Other

Name of Company / Agent

Policy Number / Amount

Policy Renewal Date

Other

Name of Company / Agent

Policy Number / Amount

Policy Renewal Date

Other

Name of Company / Agent

Policy Number / Amount

Policy Renewal Date

ELEVEN

SERVICE CONTRACTS, MAINTENANCE, AND STANDING WARRANTIES

When your family is freezing on a cold, cold weekend in January because they don't know where to find the service contract for the heating system, it's too late to say, "My bad." Your fifth-grade daughter will tell you that.

—Ralph

It's essential for your family to know where to find service contracts and standing warranties, and contact information for service and maintenance providers. You don't want to leave them trying to come up with cash to fix something that they can't live without—when you've already prepaid for the service. Or—just as bad— abandoning them to a randomly chosen repair guy or gal when you've been using a reliable person for years. If this information is all in one place and clearly marked, all the better.

Date

Automobiles
Location of Service Contracts and Warranties

Name of Company and/or Service Personnel

Email   Phone Number

Address

Name of Company and/or Service Personnel

Email   Phone Number

Address

SERVICE CONTRACTS, MAINTENANCE, AND STANDING WARRANTIES

Date _____

Recreational Vehicles (boats, scooters, motorcycles, and all-terrain vehicles)
Location of Service Contracts and Warranties _____
_____

Name of Company and/or Service Personnel _____

Email _____   Phone Number _____

Address _____

Name of Company and/or Service Personnel _____

Email _____   Phone Number _____

Address _____

Heating and Air Conditioning System
Location of Service Contracts and Warranties _____
_____

Name of Company and/or Service Personnel _____

Email _____   Phone Number _____

Address _____

House (paint, siding, roofing, chimney, fireplace, and other structures)
Location of Service Contracts and Warranties _____
_____

Name of Company and/or Service Personnel _____

Email _____   Phone Number _____

Address _____

SERVICE CONTRACTS, MAINTENANCE, AND STANDING WARRANTIES

Date _____

House (paint, siding, roofing, chimney, fireplace, and other structures) cont.

Location of Service Contracts and Warranties _____

_____

Name of Company and/or Service Personnel _____

Email _____ Phone Number _____

Address _____

Name of Company and/or Service Personnel _____

Email _____ Phone Number _____

Address _____

Name of Company and/or Service Personnel _____

Email _____ Phone Number _____

Address _____

Name of Company and/or Service Personnel _____

Email _____ Phone Number _____

Address _____

Name of Company and/or Service Personnel _____

Email _____ Phone Number _____

Address _____

Name of Company and/or Service Personnel _____

Email _____ Phone Number _____

Address _____

SERVICE CONTRACTS, MAINTENANCE, AND STANDING WARRANTIES

Date _____

Landscaping

Location of Service Contracts and Warranties _____

_____

Name of Company and/or Service Personnel _____

Email _____ Phone Number _____

Address _____

Heating and Air Conditioning System

Location of Service Contracts and Warranties _____

_____

Name of Company and/or Service Personnel _____

Email _____ Phone Number _____

Address _____

Pest Control

Location of Service Contracts and Warranties _____

_____

Name of Company and/or Service Personnel _____

Email _____ Phone Number _____

Address _____

Service Contracts, Maintenance, and Standing Warranties

Date _____

Alarm System
Location of Service Contracts and Warranties _____

_____

Name of Company and/or Service Personnel _____

Email _____   Phone Number _____

Address _____

Kitchen Appliances (refrigerator, microwave oven, range, and $1,000 juicer)
Location of Service Contracts and Warranties _____

_____

Name of Company and/or Service Personnel _____

Email _____   Phone Number _____

Address _____

Name of Company and/or Service Personnel _____

Email _____   Phone Number _____

Address _____

Name of Company and/or Service Personnel _____

Email _____   Phone Number _____

Address _____

Name of Company and/or Service Personnel _____

Email _____   Phone Number _____

Address _____

SERVICE CONTRACTS, MAINTENANCE, AND STANDING WARRANTIES

Date _____

Washing Machine and Dryer

Location of Service Contracts and Warranties _____

_____

Name of Company and/or Service Personnel _____

Email _____   Phone Number _____

Address _____

Music and Media (television, cable TV contracts, stereo, etc.)

Location of Service Contracts and Warranties _____

_____

Name of Company and/or Service Personnel _____

Email _____   Phone Number _____

Address _____

Name of Company and/or Service Personnel _____

Email _____   Phone Number _____

Address _____

Name of Company and/or Service Personnel _____

Email _____   Phone Number _____

Address _____

Name of Company and/or Service Personnel _____

Email _____   Phone Number _____

Address _____

Service Contracts, Maintenance, and Standing Warranties

Date _____

Computers, Laptops, Readers, and iPads

Location of Service Contracts and Warranties _____

_____

Name of Company and/or Service Personnel _____

Email _____   Phone Number _____

Address _____

Name of Company and/or Service Personnel _____

Email _____   Phone Number _____

Address _____

Name of Company and/or Service Personnel _____

Email _____   Phone Number _____

Address _____

Name of Company and/or Service Personnel _____

Email _____   Phone Number _____

Address _____

Name of Company and/or Service Personnel _____

Email _____   Phone Number _____

Address _____

Name of Company and/or Service Personnel _____

Email _____   Phone Number _____

Address _____

SERVICE CONTRACTS, MAINTENANCE, AND STANDING WARRANTIES

Date _____

Cell Phones

Location of Service Contracts and Warranties _____

_____

Name of Company and/or Service Personnel _____

Email _____ Phone Number _____

Address _____

Name of company and/or service personnel _____

Email _____ Phone Number _____

Address _____

Grill

Location of Service Contracts and Warranties _____

_____

Name of Company and/or Service Personnel _____

Email _____ Phone Number _____

Address _____

Other

Location of Service Contracts and Warranties _____

_____

Name of Company and/or Service Personnel _____

Email _____ Phone Number _____

Address _____

TWELVE

LOCKS AND COMBINATIONS

For security reasons, you may wish to simply record where your Locks and Combinations Record is located. Be sure to include information regarding the family safe and any other locked places or items—such as garden sheds, bicycles, gym lockers, tools and equipment, and so on.

Date

Name   Combination

Key Location

Name   Combination

Key Location

Name   Combination

Key Location

Name   Combination

Key Location

Name   Combination

Key Location

THIRTEEN

LOCKBOXES

The degree of anticipation felt by family members before opening a previously undisclosed lockbox is equaled only by an expectant mother's singular focus after her final contraction.

—Ralph

Date _____

Bank

Address

Key Location

Contents

Bank

Address

Key Location

Contents

LOCKBOXES

Author's Note

Ralph, who loves practical jokes, is the father of three children and the proud owner of three empty lockboxes.

Date _____

Bank _____

Address _____

_____

Key Location _____

_____

Contents _____

_____

Bank _____

Address _____

_____

Key Location _____

_____

Contents _____

_____

FOURTEEN

PASSWORDS

ONLINE BANKING AND INVESTING. CREDIT CARDS. Movies and photo albums. QuickBooks and Facebook. These are just a few of the Internet services that for most people are now an essential part of business and personal life.

Use the space below to record Internet sites and the usernames and passwords needed to access them. If there are passwords that you want to handle more securely by storing them somewhere like a safe or a bank security box, just let your spouse know in the space provided below where they can be found. The aim is to give the appropriate family member(s) immediate access to your accounts—when the time comes that the only password you need is the one which opens up those pearly gates!

Date

Website or URL

Username   Password

PIN

Additional Security Questions

Website or URL

Username   Password

PIN

Additional Security Questions

PASSWORDS

Website or URL

Username   Password

PIN

Additional Security Questions

Website or URL

Username   Password

PIN

Additional Security Questions

Website or URL

Username   Password

PIN

Additional Security Questions

Website or URL

Username   Password

PIN

Additional Security Questions

PASSWORDS

Website or URL

Username   Password

PIN

Additional Security Questions

Website or URL

Username   Password

PIN

Additional Security Questions

Website or URL

Username   Password

PIN

Additional Security Questions

Website or URL

Username   Password

PIN

Additional Security Questions

PASSWORDS

Website or URL

Username   Password

PIN

Additional Security Questions

Website or URL

Username   Password

PIN

Additional Security Questions

Website or URL

Username   Password

PIN

Additional Security Questions

Website or URL

Username   Password

PIN

Additional Security Questions

PASSWORDS

Website or URL

Username   Password

PIN

Additional Security Questions

Website or URL

Username   Password

PIN

Additional Security Questions

Website or URL

Username   Password

PIN

Additional Security Questions

Website or URL

Username   Password

PIN

Additional Security Questions

PASSWORDS

PASSWORDS

Part Three
Advice and Explanations

First advisory meeting

FIFTEEN

Choosing Your Advisory Teams

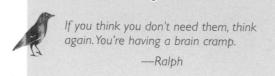

If you think you don't need them, think again. You're having a brain cramp.

—*Ralph*

ONE OF THE BEST DECISIONS YOU CAN MAKE for your spouse and children is to choose a team of advisors that they can rely on. This team can act as informal guides and a sounding board about financial and legal matters pertaining to your estate and general family concerns. You might want to have different advisors for different issues. For example, perhaps your financial advisor is the best person to help your spouse address investment concerns.

The key to the success of the advisory team is that your spouse is comfortable with your choices. If you choose people with whom your wife or husband doesn't want to talk things over, she or he is not going to go to them when it's showtime. For example, a wife may want to talk to her husband's closest friend about everything except how much money was left to her. "It's none of his doggone business! I recognize that I need help, but not from that person on this matter." That's the toned-down version of the feedback I received from my wife about one of my suggestions for our own advisors. I went back to the drawing board, and we eventually agreed on every single person. So can you.

There's an upside and a downside to forming this team. The downside is that you aren't going to be able to make any of the team meetings. The upside is that you can write a letter to the advisor/advisors, explaining to them how you want particular issues handled, so that, even in your absence, important decisions will reflect your wishes. Informal communication or handshake agreements with future advisors won't cut it, period. Why not? Because money, any amount of money, is a lightning rod for controversy. If it's not in writing, it's open to interpretation in the mind of the beneficiary—and that is a scary thought indeed.

Written, specific instructions to your advisors are especially important concerning assets and liabilities connected to potentially complicated issues. For example, my siblings and I have a verbal agreement with a neighbor who owns a beach lot adjacent to our property. If at all possible, we will try to sell his lot in combination with ours. This type of good-will agreement/obligation needs to be written down, with a clear explanation of who, what, and why. This will give your team of advisors the specific information and instructions they need.

Remember: Be clear. Be comprehensive. You've got this one shot, so don't blow it with vague directions. Choose your words carefully and repeat yourself. If you're my age or older, you already have this life skill down pat.

OUR ADVISORY TEAM

Date _____

Advisory Team Name
_____

Team Member Name
_____

Email _____ Phone Number _____

Address
_____
_____

Team Member Name
_____

Email _____ Phone Number _____

Address
_____
_____

Team Member Name
_____

Email _____ Phone Number _____

Address
_____
_____

Team Member Name
_____

Email _____ Phone Number _____

Address
_____
_____

Team Member Name
_____

Email _____ Phone Number _____

Address
_____
_____

OUR ADVISORY TEAM

Date

Advisory Team Name

Team Member Name

Email   Phone Number

Address

Team Member Name

Email   Phone Number

Address

Team Member Name

Email   Phone Number

Address

Team Member Name

Email   Phone Number

Address

Team Member Name

Email   Phone Number

Address

OUR ADVISORY TEAM

Date

Advisory Team Name

Team Member Name

Email   Phone Number

Address

Team Member Name

Email   Phone Number

Address

Team Member Name

Email   Phone Number

Address

Team Member Name

Email   Phone Number

Address

Team Member Name

Email   Phone Number

Address

SIXTEEN

Your Beneficiaries: Important Considerations

*Memories grow dim
And varying agendas abound
When reading-the-will time
Comes bounding around.*

—Ralph

TAKE A MOMENT TO CONSIDER the multitude of personal agendas through which your main beneficiaries will be filtering the information contained in *Cell Phones Don't Work in Heaven*. Your departure from terra firma is going to create a black hole, and decisions are going to be made, some sooner than others, to fill the vacuum. What are your loved ones' financial and emotional circumstances? What role will these play in influencing their thought processes and decision-making now that you are not there?

Perhaps an adult child has pressing monetary problems. If so, he or she is going to want cash and will vote for cash-producing actions at every turn. Do you want that child, particularly if he or she is in a self-made predicament, to be in a position to sway long-term financial decisions for everyone else? What about a family member or relative who might want to borrow money from your spouse now that you, Scrooge, are out of the picture?

> Knowledge of the contents of a will should be only on a need-to-know or "I want them to know" basis. Resist the temptation to reveal your will to a beneficiary with inheritance fever, even if that person contends the only cure for his or her malaise is knowing the contents of your will. Ralph counters that getting a job might ease the pain.

There might even be a long-distant cousin, with "New Wealthy Relative Syndrome," who suddenly appears and wants to be the best friend of your recently bereaved spouse. Verbal clues to this symptom include, "I've been through some rough times lately," and "I will gladly pay you back just as soon as I get back on my feet." And then to wrap up: "There's no need for a loan document; we're family."

Consider solving these issues in your will, in some form or fashion, because they will surface after you are gone. Human nature guarantees it!

SEVENTEEN

ALL ABOUT THE CHILDREN

None of us want to think about it, but remember, preparing for it doesn't make it happen.

—Ralph

IF YOU HAVE UNDERAGE CHILDREN still living at home, or a child who needs lifetime care, or even a boomerang adult child that you'd like to boomerang back somewhere, here's the place to capture the vital information they or their caregivers will need.

Date _____

Name(s) of Child or Children

_____

_____

Guardian(s)

Name _____

Email _____ Phone Number _____

Address _____

_____

Name _____

Email _____ Phone Number _____

Address _____

_____

ALL ABOUT THE CHILDREN

Date

Pediatrician

Name

Email   Phone Number

Address

Family Physician

Name

Email   Phone Number

Address

Dentist

Name

Email   Phone Number

Address

ALL ABOUT THE CHILDREN

Date _____

Orthodontist

Name _____

Email _____ Phone Number _____

Address _____

_____

Medical Specialists

Name _____

Email _____ Phone Number _____

Address _____

_____

Name _____

Email _____ Phone Number _____

Address _____

_____

Other Professional Service Providers

Name _____

Email _____ Phone Number _____

Address _____

_____

ALL ABOUT THE CHILDREN

Date _____

Other Professional Service Providers

Name _____

Email _____   Phone Number _____

Address _____
_____

Date _____

Other Professional Service Providers

Name _____

Email _____   Phone Number _____

Address _____
_____

Special Care Instructions
_____
_____
_____
_____
_____
_____
_____
_____

ALL ABOUT THE CHILDREN

Date

Special Care Instructions

ALL ABOUT THE CHILDREN

Date _____

Other Directions and Essential Information

EIGHTEEN

ELDERCARE

IF YOU ARE THE CAREGIVER OF ELDERLY PARENTS or other older relatives, here's the place to capture vital information about them.

Date

Name(s) of Elderly Parents or Other Older Relatives or Friends

Guardian(s)

Name

Email   Phone Number

Address

Name

Email   Phone Number

Address

ELDERCARE

Date _____

Physician _____

Specialty _____

Name _____

Email _____ Phone Number _____

Address _____

_____

Physician _____

Specialty _____

Name _____

Email _____ Phone Number _____

Address _____

_____

Physician _____

Specialty _____

Name _____

Email _____ Phone Number _____

Address _____

_____

ELDERCARE

Date _____

Physician _____

Specialty _____

Name _____

Email _____ Phone Number _____

Address _____

_____

Physician _____

Specialty _____

Name _____

Email _____ Phone Number _____

Address _____

_____

Physician _____

Specialty _____

Name _____

Email _____ Phone Number _____

Address _____

_____

ELDERCARE

Date _____

Location of Medical Documents

Name _____

Email _____   Phone Number _____

Address _____

_____

Location of Living Will

Name _____

Email _____   Phone Number _____

Address _____

_____

Location of Other Important Papers

Name _____

Email _____   Phone Number _____

Address _____

_____

ELDERCARE

Date _____

Special Care Instructions _____

_____

_____

_____

_____

_____

_____

_____

_____

_____

_____

_____

_____

_____

_____

_____

_____

_____

_____

_____

_____

_____

_____

_____

_____

ELDERCARE

ELDERCARE

Date _____

Other Directions and Essential Information

ELDERCARE

NINETEEN

EXPLANATIONS AND REFLECTIONS

Their life with us
and not the other way around
(we need to remember this)
their lives mingle with ours
not because they chose to
but because they have to.

We, she and I, did that to them.

Did we go too far
or not far enough?
Only the children can answer,
only the children know.

—Ralph, in a reflective mode

THE OTHER DAY I WAS STANDING IN LINE at a memorial service for a friend, talking about him with Barbara and Frank, a couple whom I have known for years. Seemingly from out of nowhere, Barbara said, "Frank, on our drive to Virginia this weekend to visit our son, I'm taking a pad and pencil so I can get your history and reflections in writing—for the children and for me."

Frank responded that he would be finished with his pearls of wisdom by the time they left their own neighborhood. But it was clear that he already knew what the topic of conversation was going to be for their trip north: him! Barbara's mind was already made up; now she was just trying to decide what color ink to use. Ralph notes that she is dead on target with this project—pun intended.

There is no better time than the present to record any cautionary notes, spiritual wisdom, or philosophical reflections that you would like to impart to your loved ones. Whether well-organized or in random fashion, write down your answers to a few of the "life moves on" questions that will face your family when you are gone. These questions are going to be addressed one way or another, with or without your input, so why not say what you think?

Do you recommend that your spouse not make any major decisions, unless absolutely necessary, for six months to a year after you are gone? Spell it out here. Do you want your family to keep the same stockbroker and insurance agent for a set amount of time? Let them know that you feel this way, and why.

And then there are the children. Do you want to leave a separate letter with advice/reflections for each of them? For those of us who are writers, this might have appeal. In fact, if you have time and interest you might want to consider a substantial volume of reflections, memoirs, or family history. For those who find such projects daunting, consider writing down just one or two sentences that capture the wisdom you want to leave behind.

Chances are you won't be able to think of everything in one sitting, so over the coming weeks try keeping a yellow pad nearby that is devoted exclusively to issues raised by *Cell Phones Don't Work in Heaven*. When something occurs to you or inspiration hits, write it down. You will be surprised by how many important subjects rise to the surface. May the Force of a pen and a clean yellow pad be with you!

Advice to Children

"Do the best you can, and don't sweat it." This is what Ralph recommends saying to your children. Isn't that what it really comes down to when raising our lovable, sometimes headache-inducing offspring? Hard not to admire Ralph's cut-to-the-chase logic on this one.

EXPLANATIONS AND REFLECTIONS

Date _____

_____

_____

_____

_____

_____

_____

_____

_____

_____

_____

_____

_____

_____

_____

_____

_____

_____

_____

_____

_____

_____

_____

_____

_____

_____

_____

EXPLANATIONS AND REFLECTIONS

EXPLANATIONS AND REFLECTIONS

EXPLANATIONS AND REFLECTIONS

EXPLANATIONS AND REFLECTIONS

Part Four
Crunch Those Numbers

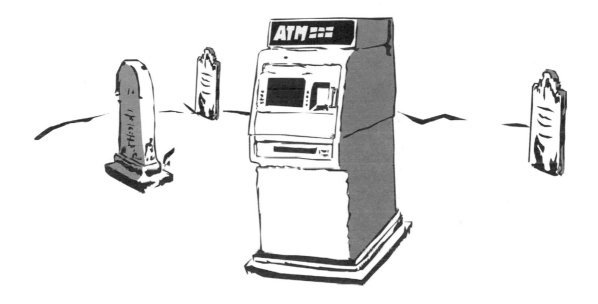

TWENTY

FORECASTING YOUR FAMILY'S GREEN $TREAM

Green, green flows the stream
It flows all the time
Even in my dreams
I love the color
I love it to death
So please don't run dry
'Til my last dying breath.

Ancient mantra from Roman Empire,
said to be chanted by happy widowed spouses.

—Translated by Ralph

IT'S TIME TO ADDRESS YOUR family's Green $tream, the long-term income stream whose hoped-for mighty flow will enable them to live with a minimum of financial anxieties. This chapter provides you with a form for estimating your family's income after you are gone. A form for estimating your family's income if you are still here but disabled can be found on pages 115–116. If you do not already know your monthly expenses, pages 80–82 will help you make an accurate estimate.

As my daughter's piano teacher used to say: Just take one page at a time and finish the drill. At the same time, if wrapping your arms around this forecast seems too complicated and mystifying to do alone, then allocate some time and money to bring in your accountant and attorney to help you figure things out.

If you come up short, at least you will know it ahead of time, and you can attack this problem in any way you see fit. One approach is to acknowledge the shortfall and tell your spouse, "Every man for himself, and by all means, keep your resume current!" Or you can take the bull by its proverbial horns and invest some energy into increasing the width and depth of your Green $tream while you still have time to do it. Remember, your Green $tream has to cover all of your bills, or some of your expenses are going to have to be reduced. It's simple math.

TWENTY-ONE

Cash, Cash, Cash

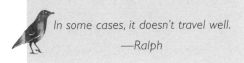

In some cases, it doesn't travel well.
—Ralph

CASH. YOU CAN'T TAKE IT WITH YOU—although I know a few people who are genuinely heartbroken by this nuance of death. Loss of life is not nearly as distressing for them as the realization that they will no longer be able to generate a net-worth figure at a moment's notice or reread their stock portfolio from the late 1990s. I digress.

Take a moment now to think through your family's potential cash crisis in the days and weeks immediately after you have left the scene. Bills are heartless, and they are going to continue showing up whether you are there or not. How will your spouse pay the mortgage and utilities, buy groceries, or cover a college tuition payment while waiting for your estate to settle? Will she or he have walking-around money? The last thing you want is for your spouse to be in a panic about cash.

You can take this problem off the table for your family right now by answering two important questions:

1. Will your partner have enough funds on hand until your estate is settled?

The answer is simple to determine by subtracting your monthly expenses (see pages 80–82 for easy-to-use forms) from the combined average monthly balance in your checking and savings accounts. If the remainder doesn't cover at least a month's expenses and preferably three, take the necessary steps to turn some long-term assets into available cash. You will be perceived as brilliant for anticipating this obvious dilemma.

2. **Will your spouse/partner have easy access to checking and/or savings accounts that have enough funds to cover immediate cash requirements?**

If the answer is no, move some assets around to make sure enough funds are immediately available. For couples with joint checking and savings accounts, or separate but equal accounts, this is not a problem. In fact, where there is sufficient trust, the easiest approach is for both partners to have access to every account, even the ones that they don't write checks on.

In some relationships, however, one person handles the finances and pays the bills, and the other person does not participate in the process. In this case, it is essential that you put in place a plan for the noninvolved spouse to transition immediately into financial responsibility. I have a friend who has always handled all the bill paying in his household, and his wife has been completely in the dark about even how to balance a checkbook. He is now helping his wife understand the ins-and-outs of financial management, so that she can transition to this new role while he is still alive.

> When it comes to ownership of money in a marriage, theoretically, there are three categories: mine, his or hers, and ours. But as Ralph astutely points out, there are really only two categories: ours and our spouse's. There is no "my" money. Ralph can't understand why I find this so puzzling.

In my own case, my wife and I have evolved a separate but equal system of checking-account management. I keep track of my account, and she keeps track of hers. My tracking method is the standard: Write down everything. Hers is more creative. She doesn't write down checks or deposits (takes too long, and why waste time writing down something you already know?) and has never reconciled a bank statement in her life. Yet she actually has a good feel about how much money is in her account. She likes to demonstrate the accuracy of her method—a little too smugly if you ask me. What can I say? Ralph advises, "Never miss a good opportunity to shut up." Ralph is a wise man.

BANK ACCOUNTS
Checking, Savings, and CDs

Date

Account Name

Location of Statements

Account Number

Type of Account   Bank Representative

Account Name

Location of Statements

Account Number

Type of Account   Bank Representative

Account Name

Location of Statements

Account Number

Type of Account   Bank Representative

Account Name

Location of Statements

Account Number

Type of Account   Bank Representative

MONTHLY EXPENSES
Household Budget

Date _____

Home	Monthly
Mortgage or Rent	$
Homeowner's / Rental Insurance	$
Property Taxes	$
Repairs / Maintenance / Homeowner's Dues	$
Furniture and Fixtures	$
Cleaning Services / Supplies	$

Utilities	Monthly
Telephone / Internet / Cable	$
Electricity	$
Water / Sewer	$
Gas	$

Transportation	Monthly
Car Payments	$
Insurance	$
Repairs / Maintenance	$
Gas / Oil	$
Other *(Public Transportation, Monthly Parking Fees, Tolls, etc.)*	$

MONTHLY EXPENSES
Household Budget

Health	Monthly
Insurance	$
Unreimbursed Expenses *(Including Dental and Vision)*	$
Fitness Programs	$
Prescription Drugs	$

Food	Monthly
Groceries	$
Eating Out	$

Clothing	Monthly
	$

Finances and Investing	Monthly
Loans and Credit Card Debt	$
Charitable Giving	$
Savings	$
Stocks and Bonds / Mutual Funds	$
IRA / 401(k)	$
College Fund	$
Alimony / Child Support	$
Emergency Fund	$

MONTHLY EXPENSES
Household Budget

Childcare / Babysitting	Monthly
	$

Vacation / Travel	Monthly
	$

Education	Monthly
School Loans	$
Tuition / Books / Fees	$

Miscellaneous	Monthly
Entertainment / Cultural Events	$
Gifts *(Weddings, Birthdays, Holidays)*	$
Hair / Personal Grooming	$
Hobbies	$
Hospitality	$
Pets	$

Other	Monthly
	$
	$
	$
	$

Total Monthly Expenses	$

GREEN $TREAM CALCULATOR

WHEN YOU HAVE FIGURED OUT your family's monthly and annual income, you will be able to answer some important questions for them. For example, after you are gone, can they afford to remain in the old homestead? Will they have to liquidate some assets to maintain their current lifestyle? If so, which assets? It is a sobering conversation to have with your spouse, but it is better to have it now while you are together than to leave him or her to answer these questions alone.

The form below will enable you to quickly calculate your family's Green $tream. Page 84 provides a space for updating this calculation if and when needed.

Ralph notes that this kind of calculation has been going on since the first caveman inventoried the rocks in his cave to make sure that he had enough to frighten away his friendly liability: the saber-toothed tiger looking for a snack.

Date _____

Funding Sources	Monthly
Surviving Spouse's Salary	$
Interest, Dividends, Capital Gains	$
Life Insurance *(Available funds after investing proceeds)*	$
Social Security / Pensions	$
Other Income	$
	$
Total Monthly Income	$
Subtract Total Monthly Expenses *(from page 82)*	– $
Green $tream Total *(plus or minus)* *(Subtract Total Monthly Expenses from Total Monthly Income)*	= $

GREEN $TREAM CALCULATOR UPDATES

Date _____

Funding Sources	Monthly
Surviving Spouse's Salary	$
Interest, Dividends, Capital Gains	$
Life Insurance *(Available funds after investing proceeds)*	$
Social Security / Pensions	$
Other Income	$
	$
Total Funding Sources	$
Total Monthly Expenses *(from page 82)*	– $

Green $tream Total *(plus or minus)*
(Subtract Total Monthly Expenses from Total Funding Sources)   = $

Date _____

Funding Sources	Monthly
Surviving Spouse's Salary	$
Interest, Dividends, Capital Gains	$
Life Insurance *(Available funds after investing proceeds)*	$
Social Security / Pensions	$
Other Income	$
	$
Total Funding Sources	$
Subtract Total Monthly Expenses *(from page 82)*	– $

Green $tream Total *(plus or minus)*
(Subtract Total Monthly Expenses from Total Funding Sources)   = $

CREDIT CARDS

*If you have more than three,
you have too many.*
—Ralph

Date

Location of Statements

Name of Card

Card Number

Expiration Date   3-Digit Security Code

Toll-free Customer Service Number

Name of Card

Card Number

Expiration Date   3-Digit Security Code

Toll-free Customer Service Number

Name of Card

Card Number

Expiration Date   3-Digit Security Code

Toll-free Customer Service Number

Name of Card

Card Number

Expiration Date   3-Digit Security Code

Toll-free Customer Service Number

CREDIT CARDS

Date

Location of Statements

Name of Card

Card Number

Expiration Date   3-Digit Security Code

Toll-free Customer Service Number

Name of Card

Card Number

Expiration Date   3-Digit Security Code

Toll-free Customer Service Number

Name of Card

Card Number

Expiration Date   3-Digit Security Code

Toll-free Customer Service Number

Name of Card

Card Number

Expiration Date   3-Digit Security Code

Toll-free Customer Service Number

Name of Card

Card Number

Expiration Date   3-Digit Security Code

Toll-free Customer Service Number

CREDIT CARDS

Date

Location of Statements

Name of Card
Card Number

Expiration Date   3-Digit Security Code

Toll-free Customer Service Number

Name of Card
Card Number

Expiration Date   3-Digit Security Code

Toll-free Customer Service Number

Name of Card
Card Number

Expiration Date   3-Digit Security Code

Toll-free Customer Service Number

Name of Card
Card Number

Expiration Date   3-Digit Security Code

Toll-free Customer Service Number

Name of Card
Card Number

Expiration Date   3-Digit Security Code

Toll-free Customer Service Number

PERSONAL LOANS

Record here your lines of credit and other related liabilities for automobiles, trucks, high-heeled shoes, deer stands, and other essential toys.

—Ralph

Date _____

Location of Documents _____

_____

Name of Toy _____

Bank _____

Email _____ Phone Number _____

Address _____

_____

Type of Loan _____

Amount Owed _____ Payment Due Date _____

Contact _____ Collateral _____

Name of Toy _____

Bank _____

Email _____ Phone Number _____

Address _____

_____

Type of Loan _____

Amount Owed _____ Payment Due Date _____

Contact _____ Collateral _____

PERSONAL LOANS

Name of Toy

Bank

Email   Phone Number

Address

Type of Loan

Amount Owed   Payment Due Date

Contact   Collateral

Name of Toy

Bank

Email   Phone Number

Address

Type of Loan

Amount Owed   Payment Due Date

Contact   Collateral

Name of Toy

Bank

Email   Phone Number

Address

Type of Loan

Amount Owed   Payment Due Date

Contact   Collateral

PERSONAL LOANS

Name of Toy

Bank

Email   Phone Number

Address

Type of Loan

Amount Owed   Payment Due Date

Contact   Collateral

Name of Toy

Bank

Email   Phone Number

Address

Type of Loan

Amount Owed   Payment Due Date

Contact   Collateral

Name of Toy

Bank

Email   Phone Number

Address

Type of Loan

Amount Owed   Payment Due Date

Contact   Collateral

DEBTS
Documented and Undocumented

Date

Location of Documents

Person / Business to Which You Owe Money

Email

Phone Number

Loan Amount

Date of Loan

Payment Schedule

Explanation

Person / Business to Which You Owe Money

Email

Phone Number

Loan Amount

Date of Loan

Payment Schedule

Explanation

DEBTS
Documented and Undocumented

Person / Business to Which You Owe Money

Email   Phone Number

Loan Amount   Date of Loan

Payment Schedule

Explanation

Person / Business to Which You Owe Money

Email   Phone Number

Loan Amount   Date of Loan

Payment Schedule

Explanation

DEBTORS
Who Owes You Money?

Date _____

Location of Documents _____

_____

Person / Business That Owes You Money

Email _____ Phone Number _____

Loan Amount _____ Date of Loan _____

Payment Schedule _____

_____

Explanation _____

_____

_____

_____

Person / Business That Owes You Money

Email _____ Phone Number _____

Loan Amount _____ Date of Loan _____

Payment Schedule _____

_____

Explanation _____

_____

_____

_____

DEBTORS
Who Owes You Money?

Person / Business That Owes You Money

Email   Phone Number

Loan Amount   Date of Loan

Payment Schedule

Explanation

Person / Business That Owes You Money

Email   Phone Number

Loan Amount   Date of Loan

Payment Schedule

Explanation

TWENTY-TWO

INVESTMENT DECISIONS

The quickest way to double your money is to fold it over and put it back in your pocket.
— A Cowboy's Guide to Life*

AFTER YOUR ESTATE IS SETTLED, most likely there is going to be cash sitting in a bank account some place that will need to be invested.

Now is the time to think about what investment strategy, if implemented, will best keep your family's income stream evergreen. If you don't take time and energy to spell this out for your loved ones, someone else will do it later, someone whose investment philosophy may be quite different from your own and whose financial competence may be questionable.

After all, who is the most quali-fied to assess all of your assets and determine what should be held, or sold now or later, to achieve your Green $tream goals? Of course, it is you—Warren Buffett's silent mentor for all these years.

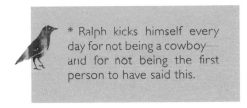

* Ralph kicks himself every day for not being a cowboy—and for not being the first person to have said this.

You probably are going to want to bring in your accountant and attorney to thoroughly analyze your family's options and opportunities. This is money well spent. Your Advisory Team should also be prepared to consult with family members around these issues after you are gone, as no matter how good your plan, "stuff happens," things change, and adjustments must be made.

INVESTMENTS
CD and Treasury Notes

If you want to have a little fun, list all of your family members as either assets, liabilities, or long-term liabilities. Nothing wrong in stirring the pot a little.

— *Ralph*

Date _____

CD and Treasury Notes

Location of Documents _____

_____

Bank Name _____

Account Number _____

Email _____   Phone Number _____

Address _____

Bank Name _____

Account Number _____

Email _____   Phone Number _____

Address _____

Bank Name _____

Account Number _____

Email _____   Phone Number _____

Address _____

INVESTMENTS
Education / College Funds

Education / College Funds

Location of Documents
_____
_____

Fund Name
_____

Account Number
_____

Email _____ Phone Number _____

Address
_____

Fund Name
_____

Account Number
_____

Email _____ Phone Number _____

Address
_____

Fund Name
_____

Account Number
_____

Email _____ Phone Number _____

Address
_____

Fund Name
_____

Account Number
_____

Email _____ Phone Number _____

Address
_____

INVESTMENTS
IRAs, 401(k)s, SEPs, Pensions, and Other Retirement Plans

My IRAs, 401(k)s, SEPs, Pensions, and Other Retirement Plans

Location of Documents

Traditional IRA   **Financial Institution / Broker**

Account Number   Symbol

Email   Phone Number

Address

Traditional IRA   **Financial Institution / Broker**

Account Number   Symbol

Email   Phone Number

Address

Traditional IRA   **Financial Institution / Broker**

Account Number   Symbol

Email   Phone Number

Address

Roth IRA   **Financial Institution / Broker**

Account Number   Symbol

Email   Phone Number

Address

INVESTMENTS
IRAs, 401(k)s, SEPs, Pensions, and Other Retirement Plans

My IRAs, 401(k)s, SEPs, Pensions, and Other Retirement Plans

Location of Documents

Roth IRA   Financial Institution / Broker

Account Number   Symbol

Email   Phone Number

Address

401(k)   Financial Institution / Broker

Account Number   Symbol

Email   Phone Number

Address

SEP   Financial Institution / Broker

Account Number   Symbol

Email   Phone Number

Address

Other   Financial Institution / Broker

Account Number   Symbol

Email   Phone Number

Address

INVESTMENTS
IRAs, 401(k)s, SEPs, Pensions, and Other Retirement Plans

My Spouse's IRAs, 401(k)s, SEPs, Pensions, and Other Retirement Plans

Location of Documents

Traditional IRA   **Financial Institution / Broker**

Account Number   Symbol

Email   Phone Number

Address

Traditional IRA   **Financial Institution / Broker**

Account Number   Symbol

Email   Phone Number

Address

Traditional IRA   **Financial Institution / Broker**

Account Number   Symbol

Email   Phone Number

Address

Roth IRA   **Financial Institution / Broker**

Account Number   Symbol

Email   Phone Number

Address

INVESTMENTS
IRAs, 401(k)s, SEPs, Pensions, and Other Retirement Plans

My Spouse's IRAs, 401(k)s, SEPs, Pensions, and Other Retirement Plans

Location of Documents
_____

_____

Roth IRA   **Financial Institution / Broker**

Account Number   Symbol

Email   Phone Number

Address

401(k)   **Financial Institution / Broker**

Account Number   Symbol

Email   Phone Number

Address

SEP   **Financial Institution / Broker**

Account Number   Symbol

Email   Phone Number

Address

Other   **Financial Institution / Broker**

Account Number   Symbol

Email   Phone Number

Address

INVESTMENTS
IRAs, 401(k)s, SEPs, Pensions, and Other Retirement Plans

Additional Retirement Plans

Location of Documents
_____

_____

Investment / Plan	Financial Institution / Broker
Account Number	Symbol
Email	Phone Number
Address	

Investment / Plan	Financial Institution / Broker
Account Number	Symbol
Email	Phone Number
Address	

Investment / Plan	Financial Institution / Broker
Account Number	Symbol
Email	Phone Number
Address	

Investment / Plan	Financial Institution / Broker
Account Number	Symbol
Email	Phone Number
Address	

INVESTMENTS
IRAs, 401(k)s, SEPs, Pensions, and Other Retirement Plans

Additional Retirement Plans

Location of Documents

Investment / Plan   Financial Institution / Broker

Account Number   Symbol

Email   Phone Number

Address

Investment / Plan   Financial Institution / Broker

Account Number   Symbol

Email   Phone Number

Address

Investment / Plan   Financial Institution / Broker

Account Number   Symbol

Email   Phone Number

Address

Investment / Plan   Financial Institution / Broker

Account Number   Symbol

Email   Phone Number

Address

INVESTMENTS
Homes and Land

Location of Documents

(Mortgage documents, warranty deed, plat, survey, insurance, house plans, etc.)

House Number One

Address

Ownership

Other Information

House Number Two

Address

Ownership

Other Information

House Number Three

Address

Ownership

Other Information

INVESTMENTS
Homes and Land

Location of Documents

(Mortgage documents, warranty deed, plat, survey, insurance, house plans, etc.)

Property Number One

Address

Ownership

Other Information

Property Number Two

Address

Ownership

Other Information

Property Number Three

Address

Ownership

Other Information

INVESTMENTS
Stocks and Bonds

Stocks and Bonds

Location of Documents

_____

_____

_____

Name   Symbol

Financial Institution / Broker

Account Number

Email   Phone Number

Address

Name   Symbol

Financial Institution / Broker

Account Number

Email   Phone Number

Address

Name   Symbol

Financial Institution / Broker

Account Number

Email   Phone Number

Address

INVESTMENTS
Stocks and Bonds in My Possession

Stocks and Bonds in My Possession

Location of Documents

Name   Symbol

Financial Institution / Broker

Account Number

Email   Phone Number

Address

Name   Symbol

Financial Institution / Broker

Account Number

Email   Phone Number

Address

Name   Symbol

Financial Institution / Broker

Account Number

Email   Phone Number

Address

INVESTMENTS
Mutual Funds

Mutual Funds

Location of Documents
_____
_____
_____

Fund Name _____ Symbol _____

Financial Institution / Broker _____

Account Number _____

Email _____ Phone Number _____

Address _____

Fund Name _____ Symbol _____

Financial Institution / Broker _____

Account Number _____

Email _____ Phone Number _____

Address _____

Fund Name _____ Symbol _____

Financial Institution / Broker _____

Account Number _____

Email _____ Phone Number _____

Address _____

INVESTMENTS
Mutual Funds

Mutual Funds

Location of Documents

Fund Name   Symbol

Financial Institution / Broker

Account Number

Email   Phone Number

Address

Fund Name   Symbol

Financial Institution / Broker

Account Number

Email   Phone Number

Address

Fund Name   Symbol

Financial Institution / Broker

Account Number

Email   Phone Number

Address

INVESTMENTS
Margin Loans

Margin Loans

Location of Documents

_____

_____

_____

Loan Number One

Bank _____

Email _____ Phone Number _____

Address _____

_____

Type of Loan _____ Collateral _____

Loan Amount _____ Due Date _____

Loan Number Two

Bank _____

Email _____ Phone Number _____

Address _____

_____

Type of Loan _____ Collateral _____

Loan Amount _____ Due Date _____

INVESTMENTS
Limited Partnerships

Limited Partnerships

Location of Documents

Description

Value

Email   Phone Number

Address

Description

Value

Email   Phone Number

Address

Description

Value

Email   Phone Number

Address

Description

Value

Email   Phone Number

Address

INVESTMENTS
Other Investments

Other Investments

Location of Documents

Name

Account Number

Financial Institution / Broker

Email   Phone Number

Address

Name

Account Number

Financial Institution / Broker

Email   Phone Number

Address

Name

Account Number

Financial Institution / Broker

Email   Phone Number

Address

TWENTY-THREE

THE DISABILITY FACTOR

One Afternoon

We played golf during his
Winding-down days
I drove the cart
And handed him his clubs
I could see
And he could feel
The Change
We didn't acknowledge it
Except once or twice we talked about the treatment.

He called his wife
Just to check in.
Just checking in, he whispered,
And how are things going?
Okay, I'll pick her up by five.

Phones without wires do wonders
For some forms of communication
But not this kind.
This was a desperate attempt by two parties
Trying to cling to normalcy
Trying to get through, not the day,
Just that one afternoon.

—Ralph

WHAT WILL BE THE IMPACT OF LONG-TERM PHYSICAL ILLNESS or mental incapacitation on your family's economic well-being? This question, in many ways, is far more complicated than making advance plans to help your family deal with financial issues in the days after your death. What if you are still around but unable to communicate? How do you develop a financial strategy for a situation with so many variables that are out of your control, including the length, kind, and cost of your medical care?

The first step is to ensure that, in the event of your incapacitation, your Advisors/Advisory Committee are prepared to consult with your family on the status of their income stream. The second step is to think through the financial consequences for your family should you need long-term hospitalization and/or nursing care. What role might supplemental or long-term care insurance play?

When you put some preliminary figures on paper, you may decide to increase the amount of your disability insurance. My guess is that your Green $tream analysis will point out that you should acquire as much long-term disability insurance as you can afford because of the unsettling uncertainty and financial burden that disability will put on your family.

GREEN $TREAM 2
Disability

The Plug

*Don't let a family member
With itchy fingers
A classic symptom of
cash-inheritance fever
Be left alone with The Plug.
Better a talkative bridge partner
Or beer-drinking friend.
You can't be too careful.*

— Ralph

Date _____

Funding Sources	Monthly
Surviving Spouse's Salary	$
Interest, Dividends, Capital Gains	$
Disability Income	$
Social Security / Pensions	$
Other Income	$
Total Funding Sources	$

Expenses Related to Disability (*estimated*)	Monthly
Out-of-Pocket Medical Expenses	$
Nursing Home	$
In-Home Nursing Care	$
Other	$
Total Disability Expenses	$
Add Monthly Expenses (*from page 82*)	+ $
Total Monthly and Disability Expenses	= $
Green $tream Total (*plus or minus*)	= $

(Subtract Monthly and Disability Expenses from Total Funding Sources)

GREEN $TREAM 2
Disability Updates

Date _____

Funding Sources	Monthly
Surviving Spouse's Salary	$
Interest, Dividends, Capital Gains	$
Disability Income	$
Social Security / Pensions	$
Other Income	$
Total Funding Sources	$

Expenses Related to Disability (estimated)	Monthly
Out-of-Pocket Medical Expenses	$
Nursing Home	$
In-Home Nursing Care	$
Other	$
Total Disability Expenses	$
Add Monthly Expenses (from page 82)	+ $
Total Monthly and Disability Expenses	= $

Green $tream Total (plus or minus) = $
(Subtract Monthly and Disability Expenses from Total Funding Sources)

PART FIVE
WHO GETS WHAT?

"Well, how else are we supposed to share it?"

TWENTY-FOUR

PRENUPTIAL AGREEMENTS

I am sure there is an argument against; I am also sure if I knew what it was, I wouldn't agree with it.
—Ralph

JACK PASSED AWAY AND LEFT HIS WIFE AND CHILDREN with a nice nest egg. His wife eventually remarried, and her new husband had a "can't-miss idea" that required seed money. He promised to pay it back with a hefty return. You can guess the rest of the story. The new business failed and took along the inheritance that Jack had worked so hard to create.

There are many versions of this story:

- You have spent years saving for a top-level education for your children, and a new marriage partner is not willing to pay the extra money needed.
- Your family's Green $tream, the one you have worked so hard to develop, gets commingled after your death with a new partner's debt-laden balance sheet.
- You and your spouse were excited about financially helping a deserving adult child as he or she heads out into the world, but a new spouse is categorically opposed to the idea.

What will happen to your hard-earned assets if your spouse gets remarried? It's a delicate but important matter for the two of you to talk over while both of you are still here. Ralph recommends against waking your spouse up in the dead of the night and expressing how you feel about that good-for-nothing future partner getting his or her hands on your hard-earned assets. Granted it might make you feel better, but your husband or wife will more than likely take exception. Just take a few moments to sit down together, perhaps while going over this book, and talk with your spouse openly and honestly about the long-term protection of your assets. Best-case scenario: You both agree to create a prenuptial agreement in the event of a remarriage.

Also consult with your attorney to make sure that your assets are adequately protected through your current will/trust structure. If not, now is the time to restructure.

Am I a little paranoid on this subject? I love you, sweetheart.

TWENTY-FIVE

Family Heirlooms

Why do relatives argue among themselves over every heirloom, whether they want it or need it? They do not want their relatives to get something they don't get for one reason only: They are relatives! Happy Thanksgiving Day dinner to all. . . .

—Ralph

ONE OF THE SMARTEST DECISIONS I ever made in my life was to take my grandfather to lunch every two weeks from the time he was eighty-five until six months before he died at the age of ninety-two.

We talked about Atlanta Braves baseball and stories from his life during the early 1900s, years he referred to as "aught three, aught four" (1903, 1904), etc. Some stories I heard over and over again, but at least once every lunch I heard something new about the "aught years" or his service as a company commander in World War I.

One day when I picked him up, he said, "Here, take this. You always liked it." It was a pocket watch given to him by the men of his command in 1919, with an inscription on the back cover. It has hung in plain sight in my dressing area ever since.

My grandfather also put stickers on a few pictures and personal items he wanted me to have after his death. Somehow, over the years, those stickers disappeared. Imagine that. . . .

Now is the time to make certain that your most precious possessions land in the hands of the right person. In the days after you are gone, when everything is in play, there are no guarantees that your wishes will be followed. Removable stickers and "Mom always said this table would be mine" carry little weight among heirs.

There are two ways to go here. Like my grandfather, you can personally give your prized possessions to a family member or friend of your choice. Or you can make a record on the following pages of your wishes. You may even want to make a record of items that you have already given away so that your family will have clarity about them.

HEIRLOOMS
And Other Designated Gifts

Date _____

Description of Gift

Recipient's Name

Email   Phone Number

Address

Description of Gift

Recipient's Name

Email   Phone Number

Address

Description of Gift

Recipient's Name

Email   Phone Number

Address

Description of Gift

Recipient's Name

Email   Phone Number

Address

HEIRLOOMS
And Other Designated Gifts

Date

Description of Gift

Recipient's Name

Email   Phone Number

Address

Description of Gift

Recipient's Name

Email   Phone Number

Address

Description of Gift

Recipient's Name

Email   Phone Number

Address

Description of Gift

Recipient's Name

Email   Phone Number

Address

HEIRLOOMS
And Other Designated Gifts

Date _____

Description of Gift
_____

Recipient's Name _____

Email _____ Phone Number _____

Address _____

_____

Description of Gift
_____

Recipient's Name _____

Email _____ Phone Number _____

Address _____

_____

Description of Gift
_____

Recipient's Name _____

Email _____ Phone Number _____

Address _____

_____

Description of Gift
_____

Recipient's Name _____

Email _____ Phone Number _____

Address _____

_____

HEIRLOOMS
And Other Designated Gifts

Date _____

Description of Gift

Recipient's Name _____

Email _____ Phone Number _____

Address _____

_____

Description of Gift

Recipient's Name _____

Email _____ Phone Number _____

Address _____

_____

Description of Gift

Recipient's Name _____

Email _____ Phone Number _____

Address _____

_____

Description of Gift

Recipient's Name _____

Email _____ Phone Number _____

Address _____

_____

HEIRLOOMS
And Other Designated Gifts

Date _____

Description of Gift _____

Recipient's Name _____

Email _____ Phone Number _____

Address _____

_____

Description of Gift _____

Recipient's Name _____

Email _____ Phone Number _____

Address _____

_____

Description of Gift _____

Recipient's Name _____

Email _____ Phone Number _____

Address _____

_____

Description of Gift _____

Recipient's Name _____

Email _____ Phone Number _____

Address _____

_____

TWENTY-SIX

WHAT'S IT WORTH?
THE PAINTING IN THE ATTIC AND OTHER VALUABLES

IN MY OFFICE, I HAVE A LIMITED-EDITION print of a tennis player by the painter Leroy Neiman that I bought thirty years ago. It's a picture my wife would never consider hanging on the wall of "her" house. Why she thinks a man caught in mid-serve shouldn't be hanging above the fireplace with a tiny little light focused on him is a mystery to me. Needless to say, this print has graced my various office walls all these years so that I can admire it out of the corner of my eye. It is worth a tidy sum, but until recently my wife didn't even know it existed—much less that it was a valuable part of our family's Green $tream. When I am gone, this expensive print might as easily end up in garage sale with a $2 price tag as in the hands of a reputable seller.

A great-aunt's necklace, a porcelain vase, an old car. Furniture, tools, artwork, and collectibles. Virtually every family has items whose worth may not be apparent to the casual observer. A good friend calls these "the painting in the attic" assets. They might be small items, like a kitchen bowl, or something big, like a parcel of land at the lake. They might not look, feel, or smell like a vital part of your family's Green $tream, but they will glow green for beneficiaries who know their true value.

On pages 127–128, record the names, descriptions, and estimated worth of those items whose existence and/or true value your loved ones are not likely to know. This record will help protect them from being taken advantage of by an unscrupulous dealer—or by other family members or friends who, afflicted with Inheritance Fever, have had their eye on that asset for a long, long time.

HIDDEN TREASURES
The Painting in the Attic and Other Valuables

Date

Item Name

Estimated Value

Description

Location of Appraisal

Item Name

Estimated Value

Description

Location of Appraisal

Item Name

Estimated Value

Description

Location of Appraisal

HIDDEN TREASURES
The Painting in the Attic and Other Valuables

Date

Item Name

Estimated Value

Description

Location of Appraisal

Item Name

Estimated Value

Description

Location of Appraisal

Item Name

Estimated Value

Description

Location of Appraisal

TWENTY-SEVEN

Planning for Pets

Enter Cat

I wasn't consulted
not even asked
I was adopted by a six-week-old cat.
Let me explain
I was a dog man from way back
My first and fattest—macho Spot,
paws on my shoulders,
a good hunting dog
snoring in my bed,
listening to my secrets,
eating ice cream from my spoon.
Real men don't like cats
because their best friends—dogs—
don't like cats.
Enter Cat.
Ever been adopted by a cat
When you don't even like them?
Better be careful.
It started slowly
Pretending not to care
She closed the trap.
Cat wore me down
I was no match for the Gaze
Couldn't resist the nose-to-nose kiss.
The random visits to my lap
Now I go to Cats Anonymous.
Hello, my name is Ralph,
and I have a problem.
I like cats.

—Ralph

MORE OFTEN THAN NOT, PLANNING for pets is an overlooked part of thinking through the future after you are gone. Of course, if your spouse and children are deeply bonded to your pet(s), and you know that they will take good care of them, you can skip this section.

If, on the other hand, you don't know how your spouse feels, or you know that there is no love lost between your partner and your pets, it's time to have a conversation. If you are single, this conversation should be with a family member or friend who can be trusted to take good care of your pet.

Because your pet's life expectancy can come into play when you are no longer in a position to take care of them, in most cases, they need a life continuance plan in place. So come up with a plan and write it down in the space provided in the following pages. You might want to call your local Humane Society for advice. Talk with friends to see if someone will agree to take your pets if you will take theirs. You might also designate funds in your will to have your pets boarded until they can be adopted. Think outside, inside, and sideways of the box on this one.

Ralph suggests that asking your pet about your spouse is the best method for figuring out if you have a problem here. Does your dog or cat pull back their ears in anticipated fear at the mere mention of living alone with your partner? Then you know what they already know: It's time to come up with a plan—and put it in writing. As always, your cold-nosed friend is counting on you.

PETS

Date

Location of Documents

Name of Pet

Name of Veterinarian

Email   Phone Number

Address

My Wishes

Name of Pet

Name of Veterinarian

Email   Phone Number

Address

My Wishes

PETS

Date _____

Location of Documents _____

_____

Name of Pet

Name of Veterinarian _____

Email _____ Phone Number _____

Address _____

_____

My Wishes _____

_____

_____

Name of Pet

Name of Veterinarian _____

Email _____ Phone Number _____

Address _____

_____

My Wishes _____

_____

_____

TWENTY-EIGHT

CHARITABLE COMMITMENTS

Camp Sunshine

Children and cancer
How can these words
Be written on the same line
Spoken at the same time
Thought about
without
an oval-shaped tear.
Yet they must be
Should be
Because there are children with cancer
And parents living with their children's cancer.
Which is worse?
Even the question brings
The tears again
In that perpetual light called your soul.

Camp Sunshine in Atlanta, Georgia, provides recreational, educational, and support programs year-round for children and adolescents with cancer and for their families.

AFTER MANY YEARS OF OBSERVING HUMAN NATURE, Ralph has astutely opined that most people are genetically programmed to be either a giver of time and money, or an "I'll get back to you" kind of person. Ralph suggests that those falling into the latter category should consider buying a seat belt for that last ride down. . . .

For those readers concerned about keeping faith with their formal and informal charitable commitments, the forms on the following pages will enable you to provide your beneficiaries with the information they need to carry out your wishes.

CHARITABLE COMMITMENTS
Obligations / Contributions without Documentation

> When you help someone who
> needs help, no questions asked,
> who is helping whom?
>
> —Ralph

DO YOU HAVE AN INFORMAL AGREEMENT to support an organization or individual? Have you promised to help a friend through a difficult time? If so, now is the time to decide if you want your family to continue with this arrangement.

Date

Name of Organization/Individual

Amount   Continue Payments?

Email   Phone Number

Explanation

Name of Organization/Individual

Amount   Continue Payments?

Email   Phone Number

Explanation

Name of Organization/Individual

Amount   Continue Payments?

Email   Phone Number

Explanation

CHARITABLE COMMITMENTS
Obligations / Contributions without Documentation

Name of Organization/Individual

Amount

Continue Payments?

Email

Phone Number

Explanation

Name of Organization/Individual

Amount

Continue Payments?

Email

Phone Number

Explanation

Name of Organization/Individual

Amount

Continue Payments?

Email

Phone Number

Explanation

Name of Organization/Individual

Amount

Continue Payments?

Email

Phone Number

Explanation

TWENTY-NINE

IF YOU OWN A BUSINESS

Willows and beneficiaries
have the same survival instincts that
sustain them through the years.
One needs water to flow to its weeping branches,
while the other needs an income stream to persevere.

—Ralph

I OWN A PRINTING COMPANY in Kennesaw, Georgia, a small city twenty minutes north of Atlanta where I have lived all my life. In my copy of *Cell Phones Don't Work in Heaven*, I have made it clear to my family that, after I am gone, I want the company to be sold in a timely way—not a fire sale, but for cash and cash only, to settle my estate.

I also have a committee set up that includes two family members, a friend, and two people from the business. They will oversee the company for my family until it is acquired, and they will also handle the sale of the company. They are authorized, if necessary, to employ someone to handle the time-consuming acquisition negotiations. The thinking behind my decision is simple: My family cannot eat a printing press, but they will be able to use the cash from the sale to solve the issue of how to find dinner and many other problems as well.

If you, like me, own all or part of a business, most likely it is a substantial portion of your net worth. As such, it is a critical factor in your family's Green $tream, and you must give it the attention that it deserves. You, to be sure, have the best handle on your business affairs, and even after your office is boxed up and cleared out, you are the one with the most insight into how best to dispose of your assets.

If you think your family members should sell the business, then tell them here. Explain in no uncertain terms why this is the most beneficial course of action for them and for the settlement of your estate. You know the growth prospects for your business, the market, the people, and the intangibles of your company. You also know the relational dynamics in your family, and by now, you also know their Green $tream requirements better than anyone else.

Ralph is a big believer in making a decision on this one and communicating your recommendation in writing so that there is no misunderstanding when your family members hold a meeting to discuss the issue. If you recommend to your family that they dispose of the business, you might also want to suggest an extended time frame for achieving this goal in order to maximize their value received—as long as it doesn't change the objective of selling the company.

If you think your family should continue to own and operate your company, explain to them why, and spell out how they can exercise oversight and control. Keeping the business in the family definitely calls for an Advisor/Advisory Team to assist family members. Consider also asking someone in the company to be on the team to facilitate monthly update meetings.

By the way, these team members are going to want to see in writing your thoughts and recommendations. They, like you, will take their charge very seriously and will welcome your input even though you can no longer physically be present to them.

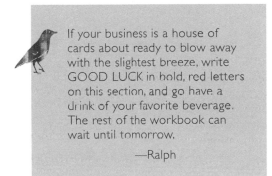

If your business is a house of cards about ready to blow away with the slightest breeze, write GOOD LUCK in bold, red letters on this section, and go have a drink of your favorite beverage. The rest of the workbook can wait until tomorrow.

—Ralph

BUSINESS
For Business Owners

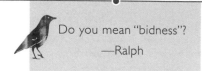
Do you mean "bidness"?
—Ralph

Date _____

Advisory Team

Name
_____

Email _____ Phone Number _____

Relationship to Business
_____
_____

Name
_____

Email _____ Phone Number _____

Relationship to Business
_____
_____

Name
_____

Email _____ Phone Number _____

Relationship to Business
_____
_____

Name
_____

Email _____ Phone Number _____

Relationship to Business
_____
_____

Name
_____

Email _____ Phone Number _____

Relationship to Business
_____
_____

BUSINESS
General Information

Date

Business Number One

Name   Ownership

EIN

Location of Stock Certificates, Minute Books, and Other Important Documents

Company Attorney (*Name and Firm*)

Email   Phone Number

Accountant (*Name and Firm*)

Email   Phone Number

Person to Call at the Company for Information

Email   Phone Number

Advisor / Advisory Team

Business Number Two

Name   Ownership

EIN

Location of Stock Certificates, Minute Books, and Other Important Documents

Company Attorney (*Name and Firm*)

Email   Phone Number

Outside Auditor / CPA at the Company for Information

Email   Phone Number

Person to Call at the Company for Information

Email   Phone Number

Advisor / Advisory Team

BUSINESS
General Information

Business Number Three

Name _____ Ownership _____

Location of Stock Certificates, Minute Books, and Other Important Documents
_____

_____

_____

Company Attorney *(Name and Firm)* _____

Email _____ Phone Number _____

Outside Auditor / CPA at the Company for Information _____

Email _____ Phone Number _____

Person to Call at the Company for Information _____

Email _____ Phone Number _____

Advisor / Advisory Team _____

Business Number Four

Name _____ Ownership _____

Location of Stock Certificates, Minute Books, and Other Important Documents
_____

_____

_____

Company Attorney *(Name and Firm)* _____

Email _____ Phone Number _____

Outside Auditor / CPA at the Company for Information _____

Email _____ Phone Number _____

Person to Call at the Company for Information _____

Email _____ Phone Number _____

Advisor / Advisory Team _____

BUSINESS
Additional Notes and Revisions

Date

BUSINESS
Additional Notes and Revisions

Date

Part Six
Final Thoughts

THIRTY

PLAN YOUR GOING-AWAY PARTY
DISCUSSING FUNERAL DIRECTIVES IS A BUMMER

INSTEAD OF PLANNING YOUR OWN FUNERAL, why not think of it in terms of a farewell party for a great guy or gal—YOU.

In the space provided on the following pages, record your essential party information: who will emcee/officiate, sing, read, speak, and so on. When choosing your pallbearers, think about your best friends who don't have bad backs. Remember there is a little heavy lifting involved.

Keep in mind that your tune selection will control the mood of the crowd, which I'm certain will be standing room only. Some might choose Verdi's *Requiem*. Personally, I'm ending my gig with the North Carolina fight song. As Ralph is fond of saying, "We are not going quietly."

> Weddings and birthdays can be repeated; this festive occasion will happen only once for you. You've got one shot. There are no trial runs.
>
> —Ralph

A part of your gala might involve a roast by a few friends and relatives. If you aren't careful, someone could reveal that checkered past that you have so deftly hidden from your spouse all these years. So take a minute to ponder which friends you want standing up and speaking and which ones you want to leave sitting down.

You see where this is going—have a little fun, plan it, and forget it.

PLAN YOUR GOING-AWAY PARTY

Date _____

Emcee / Person to Officiate _____

(Minister, Priest, Rabbi, Imam, Other) _____

Pallbearers _____

_____

_____

_____

_____

Music, Singers, and iTunes _____

_____

_____

_____

_____

_____

Readings, Readers, and Roasters _____

_____

_____

_____

_____

_____

_____

_____

_____

PLAN YOUR GOING-AWAY PARTY

Explanations and Reflections

PLAN YOUR GOING-AWAY PARTY

Explanations and Reflections

THIRTY-ONE

YOUR OBITUARY

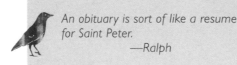

An obituary is sort of like a resume for Saint Peter.
                                    —Ralph

DID YOU KNOW THAT A LESS COMMON WORD for obituary is "necrology"? Now that's a handy piece of information to have, although I'm not sure why. It's like knowing the number 55 is a Fibonacci number—who cares? When I begin this random train of thinking, Ralph strongly suggests that I put on the air brakes before I embarrass us both. OK, done.

Why not write your own necrology so you can set the record straight about your own life? Remember, when it's needed you won't be there to defend yourself, and you can save your loved ones a lot of time and effort at a time when their hands are already full.

The website www.obituaryguide.com offers a free, comprehensive guide for creating plenty of filler for that final written curtain call celebrating your life. If you finish writing and it doesn't feel like enough, there's still time for you to accomplish some things worthy of note.

YOUR OBITUARY

Date _____

YOUR OBITUARY

Date _____

_____

_____

_____

_____

_____

_____

_____

_____

_____

_____

_____

_____

_____

_____

_____

_____

_____

_____

_____

_____

YOUR OBITUARY

Date

FINAL THOUGHTS

Date

FINAL THOUGHTS

Date

FINAL THOUGHTS

Date _____

_____

_____

_____

_____

_____

_____

_____

_____

_____

_____

_____

_____

_____

_____

_____

_____

_____

_____

_____

_____

_____

_____

KEEPING CURRENT

Making sure this book is current enables you to stay one step ahead of your beneficiaries even when you are no longer personally in the game of life. That, as the saying goes, is priceless!

—Ralph

CONGRATULATIONS! YOU HAVE TAKEN PRACTICAL STEPS to help ensure your family's Green $tream. Now you can feel confident that your loved ones will have the information they need in a time of momentous change and transition.

But remember, your financial situation and personal relationships will continue to evolve and change, and this document is not meant to be static. Like your life itself, it is a work in progress and needs to be periodically reviewed. Is the information inside these pages accurate and up to date? Does it reflect your current thoughts and wishes?

Take a moment now to establish a semiannual review date of your *Cell Phones Don't Work in Heaven* documents and put it on your calendar. It's like your personal life goals—if you don't write them down and constantly review them, they aren't going to happen. During your semiannual review, use the time to read over your will, trusts, and all other provisions concerning your beneficiaries.

May your life, and the lives of those you love, be long, illustrious, and full of love!

About the Authors and the Artist

Mark C. Pope is a businessman, husband, and father whose own interest in documenting his family's assets began with a potentially fatal accident. His career includes a stint as an officer in the U.S. Navy and serving as president of a publicly held company. Today he is the owner and president of Graphic Solutions, Inc., a graphic communications company. He serves on numerous nonprofit boards and lives in Atlanta, Georgia, with his family.

Barbara R. Thompson is an award-winning writer and writing coach who lives in Atlanta, Georgia, and Brevard, North Carolina.

Roger Fleming is an illustrator and designer living in Atlanta, Georgia.

Special Sales/Bulk Sales/Premiums
For information about bulk sales for nonprofits, civic groups, book clubs, faith communities, extended families, and other organizations, please contact Mark Pope at popepub@gsghome.com.

www.cellphonesdontworkinheaven.com